EVERYTHING YOU WANT TO KNOW ABOUT

COURT REPORTING

(And a few secrets, too)

Choose the stenotype machine, the GOLD STANDARD

WOULD YOU LIKE TO EARN A 6-FIGURE INCOME FAST?

MARIJANE STOMBERG

Copyright © Marijane Stomberg 2022

All rights reserved. No part of this book may be reproduced, scanned or transmitted in any forms, digital, audio or printed, without the expressed written consent of the author.

Cover Page by: Proven Results Marketing

Cover Page Speed Emblem by: Klor & Legal Grins

Cover Page Court Stenographic Reporter Emblem by: Legal Grins

EVERYTHING YOU WANT TO KNOW ABOUT

COURT REPORTING

(And a few secrets, too)

Choose the stenotype machine, the GOLD STANDARD

WOULD YOU LIKE TO EARN A 6-FIGURE INCOME FAST?

MARIJANE STOMBERG

DEDICATION

I would like to dedicate this book

to

My Paternal Guardian Grandparents

Ernest and Catherine Vollmar

for teaching me personal drive and independent responsibility

and

My adult children, **Jennifer Stomberg Walker, and Karl Stomberg***, who have demonstrated the attributes of personal drive and exceptionalism I had hoped for them. My son and daughter continue to be my daily inspiration, along with all my grandchildren.*

CONTENTS

                                                                                Page No.

Chapter 1

My Reason for Writing This Book 1

Chapter 2

Sitting in the Court Reporter's Chair 4

Chapter 3

Taking a Tort (And I don't Mean Chocolate Mousse) 18

Chapter 4

A Sudden Turn to the Emotional Involvement:

What to Do if the Witness Starts to Cry 20

Chapter 5

"Do I have What It Takes to Be a Court Reporter?" 23

Chapter 6

You Can Handle It 36

Meet Dollie Doppelganger, the Voice in My Head 37

Never Quit! 42

Page No.

Chapter 7

Starting Out - Practicing in Court or in Depositions.............. 44

Chapter 8

Additional Helping Aids 46

Chapter 9

Proper Behavior, Manners in Court, or a Deposition 48

Chapter 10

The Signed Court Reporter's Certificate 49

My Wish For You 49

A Rhythmic Cadence Of Its Own Vitality.............................. 51

Chapter 11

Would you like to earn a 6-Figure Income?.......................... 55

CHAPTER 1

MY REASON FOR WRITING THIS BOOK: GIVING BACK

Why have I written this book? To introduce you to the exceptional profession of Court Reporting, to tell you what it is, what it takes to be one, and how to become one. I am proud of having been a court reporter. I enjoyed this extremely interesting profession for over four decades; one that paid well and provided me with a high standard of living, and brought me into contact with wonderful associates, colleagues, officials within the judicial and legal realms. It is now time for me to give back by sharing important highlights of what I have learned and encouraging others to enjoy court reporting, too. You may have some information about this profession, and you may have a great curiosity about it and all that it entails, but your scant review may lead you to believe, "Oh, no, I could never do that…, but I sure would like to try!" Or "I wonder, could I ever do that?" Relax, I am here to help you. Help is on the way! I offer here my message. You will love the next news I give you. Read on!

Court Reporters are in demand! The supply of them does not meet the demand. There presently is a shortage of verbatim court reporters which is unfortunate for several reasons, but most importantly, because many people are losing out on the chance to be involved in a truly marvelous and satisfying profession. You may ask, "Why do people not flock to fill these available positions?" Because until my book arrived, "Everything You Want To Know About **COURT REPORTING** (And A Few Secrets, Too)," there has not been a thrilling, imaginative, compelling, or insightful look into this profession until now. Once people find out what a court reporter's life is really like, they will flood the gates of the court reporting schools to get in and prepare for those positions.

The reason people do not know what goes on in the court reporter's inner mind is because, by and large, that has not been shown. Her/his feelings have not been memorialized in the huge part that a CSR, Certified Court Reporter, plays in the proceedings in our legal world. They, frankly, have been invisible in the chronicling of the legal realm. There has been little mention of the crises that have occurred to the CSRs on their watch, no accounting for the effect that years of long hours of dedication to the work that they have put forth in performing the most important and needed role of their professional life has had on them, personally, and, most outstanding, the crucial role the court reporters play in the execution of their most important procedure performed in the courtroom, and that is the rendering of the Reporter's Record, a verbatim transcript of every word spoken in the process of making the stenographic record of the matters before the court.

Until now. I lived the life of the myriad facets of the court reporter's role, both in the free-lance world and the official court reporter's world, and after almost 45 years of being part of this wonderful industry of perpetuating the continuity of the individual voices spoken under the jurisdiction of our laws, I write this informative book to give the public insight into the "no longer invisible" noble protectors of The Record.

CHAPTER 2

SITTING IN THE COURT REPORTER'S CHAIR

To help you understand what is involved that enables you to take the chair of the Court Reporter, I am delighted to offer my assistance in explaining the profession of court reporting to you in a very forthright, straight-forward manner so you can get a sense of what it is like to "wear the hairshirt of the crusader" in the production and protection of The Reporter's Record which you would seek to do in this profession as you consider making it your own. This is a noble profession, and you will be noble for pursuing it. It has the endearing characteristic of bringing out the best in people. You will come to realize what a gift you are to the community.

"**Wearing the hairshirt of the crusader**" means you will protect, fight for, and have great reverence for the product you are producing, the **verbatim Reporter's Record**. That is very substantial in that you will have taken an oath to do so, and many people are counting on you to provide this product which will be forever encased in the legal cases throughout history, and you will be doing the chronicling of its verbatim history.

It is most important to note and be very aware that no one can presume to be a court reporter who is not qualified, not educated in it, not certified and not honorably regarded as a court reporter, or to present oneself as a certified court reporter when one is not, because that is against the law; it is at least a misdemeanor and one committing such a fraud upon the public will have to face a trial and severe circumstances if this fraud is committed. So, live by the rules established and be the honest person you are, and you will be highly honored in this great profession. The schools teaching this occupation today are highly credible and have all the information you need to share with you. Just be sure that you opt for a school that Is accredited by the National Court Reporters Association which you will find as a most beneficial asset.

> Note: For your information, I offer this small portion of the ruling on this point

By the Supreme Court of Texas (because I have gained most of my court reporting

Experience in Texas) However, for all of you living in other states, just pull up

The Supreme Court of your state via the Internet, Google, etc., and search for

Rules governing **Court Reporting**, and it will most likely be very similar.

IN THE SUPREME COURT OF TEXAS: MISC. DOCKET NO. 11-9081, 04/26/2011.

It is ORDERED THAT: "Pursuant to Chapter 52 of the Texas Government Codes,

This Court approves the following Rules Governing Court Reporting Certification and Court Reporting Firm Registrations:

"Court reporting" and "shorthand reporting" mean the practice of shorthand

Reporting for use in litigation in the courts of this state by making a **VERBATIM**

RECORD of an oral court proceeding, deposition, or proceeding before a grand

Jury, referee, or court commissioner using written symbols in shorthand, machine

Shorthand, or oral stenography."

Consequently, my purpose in writing this book is to motivate and inspire interested job seekers to enter the wonderful profession of court reporting by stenographic method, this Gold Standard for reporting; also called machine touch shorthand, whose unique purpose is to render a verbatim transcript of proceedings had, held in a courtroom or deposition suite, which written record is a vital tool for judges, attorneys, and their parties involved in litigation; and to encourage interested people to enter an area where there is now a strong demand for court reporters far beyond what was anticipated, and one which pays very well.

My book seeks to give inspiration, motivation, and educate future court reporting students on what the life of a court reporter is all about. I want them to see it from the actual chair of the court reporter, what she/he hears and types on this small machine with only 22 keys on it. This one-of-a-kind Stenograph machine is like a typewriter, as having keys you depress, but immensely different in that it is multifaceted. You will be typing words in one stroke, phrases in one stroke, and you will learn to type with a rhythm that will develop as you learn your skill that will feel comfortable. You will feel more confident every day, building to your final objective of writing automatically. At that point you will feel the moment yearned for – the epiphany of, "It has finally happened. I feel like my fingers are 'Dancing on the Keys!'" By the time you get to the courtroom or the deposition suite, you will be thoroughly prepared. Because of the tremendous strides in technology over the last 50 years, especially, which is all available for your knowledge and convenience, you can now produce a print-out transcript of the hearing in the courtroom or deposition suite in real-time fashion, which means "immediately," or on-the-spot. Most of the time the real-time print-out will be considered a rough draft with a disclaimer stating as such, until a careful re-read is done to correct any typos or misspellings, at which time it becomes the "ORIGINAL."

The courtroom is the theater of life. You will see and hear major events of one's life involving contracts, trusts, disloyalty, crimes. Just about every event can have a legal twist, result, or need a clarification legally from a judge or jury.

I want to show you and those interested what a marvelous profession this is and how you can overcome the seemingly insurmountable obstacles you will meet along the way in conquering this skill and learn how to overcome those obstacles.

Yes, it is a great skill you are developing and one that will require constant dedication and constant practice. However, when you look at the end of the tunnel, keeping your eye on your main objective – success as a court reporter –you will stay focused and WILL BECOME a court reporter. You must from Day One see yourself in school as a court reporting student, and then in the chair in court or in a deposition suite as a Certified Court Reporter! Seeing it is believing it. Please do not be timid or fear anything about this profession if you really have a desire to learn more. That's why I am here right now -- to educate you right here in this book about a truly fabulously interesting work that has so many pluses, and, yes, it is entirely doable for you if you really want it. Some of what I offer here will not be pointed out to you in the school you choose as they are things I learned in my experiences as a fledgling student and then as a working court reporter for over forty-five years. Also, each state will have a little different approach to the "what and when" of learning this skill, but I speak to you in a general sense.

I also want you to realize that you will witness many of the emotions people feel, as a court reporter works through and observes the trials and tribulations testified to in the witness's testimony and the circumstances surrounding them.

Please be very aware of the importance and value of the Reporter's Record. The court reporting profession has always been one of the greatest assets to the judges presiding over our courts and to the legal community in which the attorneys use our product, our invaluable verbatim transcript, the Reporter's Record. They value the certified transcript's existence that enables the attorneys and judges to study the evidence, the printed-out text and testimony, and the attorneys will argue their cases on it, and the Reporter's Record will help attorneys win their cases on appeal. They view the transcript's existence as a primal force enabling them to do so even on a real-time, instant print-out basis. Even the jurors sitting in the jury box derive invaluable assistance from the court reporter when they may request the reporter to read back portions of testimony they need to better understand as to a particular point in the testimony. Realize how important the Record is to all involved – not just you – but the attorneys, the judge, the litigants. You are providing a great service which the attorneys are also paying for when ordering the transcript from you.

The Reporter's Record is not just a transcribed, printed document. It is a verbatim transcript, word-for-word, of proceedings had in open court or in a deposition including sworn testimony taken of witnesses who are given an oath to testify to the truth of the matter then before the Court, according to the rules of law regarding perjury. This is a very serious matter and one which everyone who is concerned with the matter gives great gravitas, especially, the court reporter who puts her honor in the certificate she signs.

Grooming yourself for this position will create tremendous personal growth in you. The same personal fight we have with preparing to enter this profession is the same fight one would have to encounter in whatever profession they choose so that they may be successful, and that is: Realize your goal and take the necessary steps to get there; hone up on your personal characteristics of perseverance, tenacity, and discipline. There are mountains to climb in any field one would choose and getting there is simply taking the steps, one at a time, over the mountain to get there and achieve success. Believe in yourself. If it has been done by others, it can be done by you!

Be inspired. Be motivated. Your life will change in many ways, I guarantee you, when you become a CSR, Certified Shorthand Reporter. You are going to be very proud of yourself when you achieve that goal because you will possess a highly valued and needed, unique skill, one that is in demand, and you will enjoy a very lucrative profession, enabling you to enjoy an enhanced lifestyle. You can do it!

I'm thinking about you, the people who are interested in court reporting and are reading my eBook, or rushing to buy the audio version, my paperback or hard copy book right now.

I am wondering where you are in life. You may be a student in high school or college who is looking for a new challenge in entering an established livelihood, a job, a good earning for your hard work and dedication, of such significance that it would rally you forward to learn more and more until it truly becomes an infatuation for you. Because it is true: That the more you learn about the court reporter's place in the courtroom and all the fascinating happenings around her/him, the more you cannot put this book down. Trust me, you are going to love reading about it. As a matter of fact, you may also feel the need to buy the paperback book just to have it close by to keep your inspiration lit and your confidence strong!

Interestingly, a friend of mine, Nora, was a court reporter, and when she started to have children, she decided to retire from it for a while, but felt she would someday return to reporting. That's exactly what Nora did. Once the children had completed high school, she went back to a court reporting school to refresh her skills, pulled out her old dictation tapes and Stenograph machine, and then after about six weeks' refreshing, she jumped right back into substituting as a Deputy Official Court Reporter in various courts in California. It did not take long at all for her to realize the courts needed her and her skills because of the demands in the field. At this point, Nora was in her fifties, and she was living the good life, feeling needed again professionally and she was one happy lady because the additional, very substantial income she now made again allowed Nora to pay the college costs for her children.

Then there are my friends, Jake, and Karen, who were just married and while Jake was very well off financially in his new business, Karen decided she would continue her court reporting education so they could afford to buy a house sooner, decorate and furnish it, and still enjoy their frequent vacations without feeling financially pinched. She decided to work at court reporting part-time which she found to be a more comfortable routine for her.

At this point I want to stress that this profession invites men and women. Both genders are heartfully accepted and needed, and that also includes everyone. All administrators care about is that you are a licensed professional with the honored ability of writing the Reporter's Record accurately and delivering it expeditiously. There are many men who are court reporters, and they are among the very best as well as women.

And they make great friends and fun friends! A reporter is judged only by her/his Record and how quickly they can deliver it to the person ordering it. I have heard from some judges that it matters not whether his/her court reporter is a woman or a man, but in one case I know of, a judge's wife suggested that she would feel more comfortable if he hired a man reporter. Spousal happiness intervened in this instance.

There are many other perks that will be revealed to you as we progress along. Read, learn, and enjoy!

After over forty-five years of working in this field as a free-lance court reporter and also at different times as an official court reporter, working for one judge, one court, I can tell you, yes, the work was very hard, very difficult at times with expert testimony, with concentrating diligently on the various worldwide accents you must train your ear to hear, and the never-ending deadlines you must meet, and always at the forefront is your concerted effort to strive for excellence in an effort to please the judges and attorneys that you are working with at that moment by giving them the most accurate, expeditious transcript possible which must be verbatim. But it was also the most exciting profession to me for so many reasons.

From the first day of writing as an employed Certified Court Reporter, I worked with smart, wonderful, dedicated people. My peer CSRs (Certified Court Reporters) were great people of noble intent, and I always considered it an honor to work for the fine judges and the dedicated attorneys. I was part of the beauty of the court system, the legal system, and felt how most everyone passing through the courtroom doors did honor this juggernaut, this symbol for justice in American life, and you could feel their reverence. I knew I was providing a service to my community, and I felt proud that I could help to be of assistance in such an important area of our world and still be paid so highly for it.

I loved the excitement of the trials, observing the pure talent of the various attorneys arguing the case for their litigants, whether it be a criminal or a civil trial, noting how the judge rules on the objections that usually come in fast and furiously in a sometimes feisty trial, and I was always amazed at the proficiency of manner in which judges could make their ruling so quickly, on-the-spot so often, because they had a great knowledge of the law governing the case. You learn fast why judges and able attorneys receive so much respect. They deserve it. We live in the greatest country in the world when realizing that we have the fairest jury system in the world to be so grateful for. While not perfect, we are lucky to have it, because it is the best thing going for Americans, legally.

CHAPTER 3

TAKING A TORT (AND I DON'T MEAN CHOCOLATE MOUSE!)

Imagine, you are a court reporter, and it is your first day to take a tort in court. Your mind may conjure up a vision of a chocolate mousse torte being handed to you by food guru Julia Childs, but, alas, not so. The reality is you are there to report a hearing about a wrongful act or infringement of a right that someone committed, leading to civil legal liability.

Thus begins your preparation of The Record for that day. A hearing can be a trial, or a separate hearing in which some transgression, trespass, abuse has occurred, and it has led to a lawsuit. The attorneys are depending on you, the writer, the producer, and the protector of The Record, to accurately report the Proceedings on your stenographic machine, and that means verbatim, word for word. But no problem here, because you will have worked hard, have studied ferociously to attain the talent and ability, phalangeal agility, to do this job; you have received your certification giving you license to do so by the Governor's Office or license-governing body of your state. Now, you have made it, having achieved these skills, and you are proud of your accomplishment.

Still, your knees are a little shaky, your hands a little clammy. You have taken on so much responsibility to so many people. You think, "Can I do the job?" Relax. We all think of that when starting out. You have covered all your bases. You are finding that it's much different when you are no longer writing in a class and the instructor gives you his smiles of approval and the students are your friends. However, you are in a huge courtroom now with strangers you have never seen before, an intimidating, all-knowing judge, powerful, brilliant attorneys, and perhaps a jury of people who are looking at you, seemingly mesmerized by the small machine your fingers are moving over which doesn't seem to make any noise. This is even before the witnesses take the stand and emotions begin. Yes. Emotions are very often part of the trial or hearing and you have to deal with them.

CHAPTER 4

A SUDDEN TURN TO THE EMOTIONAL INVOLVEMENT: WHAT TO DO IF THE WITNESS STARTS TO CRY

IMAGINE: You are a court reporter and it's your first divorce case, and it is grueling. The people, who at a time before had professed eternal love for one another, are now seeing the other in a totally unfavorable and often even a vicious light. The woman, destroyed by the marriage-gone-wrong, disseminated into a flood of tears, sobbing.

What does the court reporter do? She, in a very smart forethought, had placed a box of Kleenex in front of the witness's chair, quickly hands her one and, never pausing, continues to write down the witness's testimony. YOU DO NOT STOP WRITING.

What happens if the court reporter starts crying? I assure you, this will happen, especially if the case involves children, child abuse, criminal cases, divorces. So, prepare yourself.

THE COURT REPORTER KEEPS ON WRITING! The writing continues until the judge states, "We'll go off the record for a moment." It is within the judge's purview only to give instructions of going ON and OFF the Record.

Allow me to relate an experience I had. My first month in District Court, in a criminal case I was reporting, two young teenagers, two brothers, were convicted of armed robbery with intent to harm, and at the sentencing for their crime, the two young men, good-looking and were both crying, begging for leniency, asking for another chance, saying that they were very sorry for their crimes, and I, as I continued writing all this, began crying myself for these misled youths; yet, knowing that the most important thing for me at that moment was to keep writing, to not stop the serious flow of the vital testimony. And, although I was nearly sobbing loudly, I continued writing to the end. Unfortunately, because of the seriousness and nature of what

21

these boys were involved in, the judge sentenced them to ten years in prison, and they were immediately incarcerated. These beautiful young men would live locked up, under constant guard. I was depressed for weeks afterwards because of the absolute loss these boys and their families would encounter, would feel, and how that one nefarious night of crime had ruined the lives of so many close to them as well as themselves.

A court reporter learns early on that she must not allow herself to get emotionally involved in a case, but, frankly, it took me years to learn that much control.

CHAPTER 5

"DO I HAVE WHAT IT TAKES TO BE A COURT REPORTER?"

You are thinking, "How do I know if I have what it takes to be a court reporter?"

Let's get down to some basic facts. Let's make this simple.

To be a court reporter you need:

1. <u>A good understanding of the English Language</u>, most of which you get the basics of by high school graduation. You must be able to spell and know accurate grammar and punctation. Note: your vocabulary will continue to grow with each trial while you are in court; especially, if you endeavor to journal specific words related to the trial and you commence to use them in your conversation.

   You will always be improving your verbal knowledge and verbal ability throughout your career as a court *reporter. Also, you will be in a continuum of learning, in the best way, really, because you are learning through the real-life situation of the trial of the matter which is revealed before you in the Reporter's Record as you write. I found this to be vastly interesting. Some cases were so interesting, I wanted to just stop writing and listen.*

I feel a strong need to point out here an emphasis of the power of attorneys, the learned attorneys, the evocative characteristic that exists in their voice, when they speak beautifully in their arguments to the judge, or in their statements, arguments to the jury. I, as a court reporter of many years, relished and appreciated their knowledge of the proper phraseology, tone, talent and presentation, persuasiveness to the jury. To me, when well done, it was beautiful theater; it was their passion and belief in their fight for justice for their client that permeated the courtroom. It drew attention. It held power.

From the court reporter's chair, you can see not only the attorney's comportment, but also the faces of the jury and you might catch a hunch of how persuasive the attorney's argument is.

So, you see, contrary to an impression that the court reporter is a stoic robot, with a disinterested expression on her/his face, the court reporter is thinking every second, concentrating intensely.

Words are being processed rapidly which she is writing quickly and astutely, but the reporter is also able to understand the words and theory behind the words and their effect on the listeners. The reporter is writing automatically, but always with a subconscious awareness to each stroke and that is a wonderful accomplishment of the human brain. When you think about it, we are an incredible species.

2. <u>Dexterity of fingers</u>. Note that any typing you do on a typewriter or computer are necessary and great for dexterity. Try to achieve a typing speed on a regular typewriter of 80 wpm at least. Remember, when you go to take your CSR

Exam, you only have a short time to transcribe each dictated section. You must be prepared. If you are allowed to bring your computer for translation, great. Otherwise, you will be offered a typewriter to transcribe it on. At the Exam, you will need time to proofread for grammatical and punctation errors, too. The test must be letter perfect. My friend, Anne, had a very disappointing experience. She flew through the stenographic writing part of the exam and felt very complacent that she got it all down in stenotype. However, when she went to transcribe on a regular typewriter all that she had written, Anne could not get it typed up fast enough before the bell rang, and she could not get the test handed in on time simply because her typing speed on the regular typewriter was not good enough to finish and pass. Very unfortunate. Don't let this happen to you. Normally, you only have a chance to take the examination every six months.

> One good thing concerning your dexterity is if you have had any lessons in piano, that is a helpful asset, and you already have great dexterity. Typing also builds dexterity. Many of you will be quite proficient on your desktop computer or laptop by now.

> *As an interesting note, in reading my JCR Magazine, the November, 2021 issue published by the NCRA, there was a story about Janine Ferren, a court reporter, RMR, CMR, who also had a second degree in classical piano, and in winning an audition during her sophomore through senior years was chosen to play in three performances at Carnegie Hall in New York City. Her finger dexterity had to be supreme! Very Outstanding, Janine.*

3. <u>Enroll in a NCRA (National Court Reporters Association)-Accredited Court Reporting School</u>

> *Study the textbooks which the school will have on the human body, skeleton, engineering terminology, medical terminology, legal terms, and different vernaculars for different fields. You will also learn the ins and outs of court reporting, how to build a dictionary for real-time translation, long vowels, abbreviations, and the whole gamut involved. It is not necessary to have a 4-year degree, but it is very important to absorb all the knowledge available for the court reporting profession that your school offers.*

I am a strong proponent on finishing the program on your own merit. Some students can learn all they need in two years' time; some even less to be qualified to take the CSR tests and pass. It is all up to you.

4. *Dexterity for speed is very important. The best way to build speed is to push for higher speed by – what do you think?*

   Answer: REPETITION!

   Some informed and driven students can build their own skills faster than others and will not take as much time acquiring those skills. One's level of progress when beginning this course will be determined by (1) the general knowledge and common sense they have already gleaned from life and school, and (2) their drive, their tenacity and perseverance they possess in their desire to succeed.

5. *Reviewing your Latin word foundations will be taught so you can figure out many words that are spoken. Also, learning about the "ologies" as in dermatology (study of dermatology) and "itises" as in dermatitis (inflammation of the skin). These endings in medical terms will give you a great familiarity with word meanings.*

While medical terminology is challenging, there is a method to understanding it and I found it to be the most interesting testimony. Doctors make great witnesses, are most cooperative in speaking clearly for the court reporter. If you do not understand something, the good thing is that you will write it phonetically which will help you to correctly research the word later for the correct spelling. You may refer to documents in the file or the exhibits in the case or on the Internet which are welcome sources.

NOTE: If you do not understand a word or phrase that a witness speaks, it is important that you stop the witness and ask him to repeat it. Be quick and courteous, and you could say, "I'm, sorry, could you repeat that?" The witness will usually be happy to oblige because they want a correct transcript, also, as well as the attorneys.

Remember, interrupt only when necessary, so that you are not disrupting the questioning attorney's line of thought or the witness's. You can get most all spellings from the briefs in the file or the Notice of the Deposition. You do not want to ask a witness about any spelling you can get out of available sources and research books. Prepare a Job Dictionary before the hearing day or deposition, if possible. That will be invaluable. If you go in cold to a hearing with no time to read the file, do not fret. You will find that you will learn about the case the moment the attorneys begin speaking on the record and they will repeat many of the proper nouns so that you will quickly pick up who the people are, and the subjects involved.

Once the hearing or trial starts, you will gain instant familiarity with the vernacular of the matter and will find yourself creating your own Job Dictionary on the spot. Our current technology is so superior.

6. <u>*Your second-most important goal*</u> *during learning the textbook material also is, concurrently,* <u>*building your speed on the machine*</u>*; that means writing every single day, writing fast Motions, Question and Answer tapes, Jury Charge, Literary, and the best way to achieve speed is to write the News on*

TV! Very important. Newscasters talk very fast – sometimes 325 wpm --and it is very, very difficult to take down. Then write something else on TV at slower speeds. This is the best speed builder by far. Your machine is now your closest friend. Respect what it can do in your hands, and it will serve you well. Write every day. Here is the most important thing and do the following with great discipline: Every day read back some of the most difficult dictation you took when practicing. You see, you must train your eyes to recognize the stenotype you are writing. The one great asset, you will find, is writing your long vowels in the words. That makes reading back so much easier! My readback was outstanding because I disciplined myself from the beginning to readback portions of what I was writing, and always maintained that crucial habit.

> *I know it is very common to want to write as fast as possible as quickly as possible but the reality is that you need to know very well the textbook material – not that you are learning to be an engineer or a doctor, but it is priceless that you read and hear these really difficult multi-syllable words that you are hearing phonetically, writing phonetically, and*

then developing a familiarity with them which, with repetition, ingrains them into your brain. So, here you have your first secret:

Secret No. 1: <u>Repetition.</u> This is the key to mastering the skill of court reporting via machine shorthand. Repetition. Over and over. It seems almost too simple to realize. You will learn to incorporate a fluctuation in this method as you read on.

Think back to when you were in elementary, secondary school, and remember how you learned about the subjects reading, writing and arithmetic. By repetition. You wouldn't normally get things on the first read, but if you read it again, you would; and the more difficult the terminology or problem, the more times you had to repeat your reading of it. So, it is the same with writing the phonetic language on a new machine, the Stenograph. You are training your mind to hear, decipher, abbreviate, and make the nerves in your brain transfer all that to your fingers which you are moving around on the machine writer, reaching in a myriad of positions and contortions to create these words in print and on paper *and laptop/computer, digitally. The best thing about writing phonetically is that it eliminates writing excessive letters one does not really need to figure out the word. E.g., weight = wat, using the long "a" as in waeut. For clarification, the vowel "i" in steno is identified as "eu". We are grateful for these time savers, right?*

7. <u>When you are at 180, find a mentor in court</u> *or in an agency, another court reporter, or just politely approach an official court reporter and ask if you can sit in her court as a reporting student for practice for a few weeks. She will know that once you become certified, she can use you as a substitute when she needs days off herself for a vacation or to produce an appellate transcript. You cannot legally work as a court reporter unless you are properly licensed. To do so is a misdemeanor and can have brutal results, plus forever forbidding you to work as a court reporter again.*

8. <u>Go for your Certification Examination for a license to be a court reporter</u>. *Be prepared so you can pass it on the first go-around. Be organized, anticipate what you need to know and do to pass the exam. Do not be surprised. Know the logistics and locations of the examination location before you leave your house. Rethink all logistics and plan accordingly.*

9. *Be relaxed and confident. You can do this.*

10. *As early as possible, after you have begun your training, I strongly suggest you <u>acquire a subscription to JCR Magazine (Journal for Court Reporting)</u> published by NCRA (National Court Reporters Association), a great organization which is of magnificent assistance to beginning students as well as to all levels of court reporters and it is a massive source for just about anything having to do with court reporting and other related methods of recording data.*

    NCRA offers a discounted subscription for students, you will be happy to hear, and it is indeed a great asset to have at your fingertips, if you'll pardon the pun!

    NCRA publishes JCR, Journal of Court Reporting, a national magazine, so it highlights where there are jobs available in the nation.

    As a rather adventurous person myself, I always loved the idea of being able to work anywhere I wanted in my country – the United States – because there has always been a steady demand for court reporters all over and I knew with my experience, I could get a job quite easily. I always was attracted to the bigger cities like New York, Los Angeles, Houston because their need for court reporters was even greater and that correlated to a chance for a larger income. I began reporting in Detroit, Michigan, then I moved to Houston and worked extensively there and enjoyed a flourishing business as both a free-lance and official court reporter.

Then later, when my children went to college, I decided to move to Los Angeles, CA, where I had always wanted to work in their Superior Court. I passed the required examinations and had an exciting, delightful, most lucrative four years of working there. The great thing about working in the Los Angeles court system is that it was very well-organized, and many of the courthouses were either on the oceanfront or close to the ocean, like around Santa Monica and Huntington Beach. I thought I was in heaven!

CHAPTER 6

YOU CAN HANDLE IT!

Finally, you passed the examinations, and you have become a licensed, certified court reporter. You can handle it. How do I know that?

Because you have trained for it. Because you've gone the distance. Because you persevered. Because you knocked down every one of the barriers and focused on erecting the building blocks of skill, knowledge, speed, determination, energy, self-motivation, drive; drive for a better life, a better job, a better "place to grow". Because you never stopped believing that you could do this, and you did it.

* * * *

Up to this point I have given you a very condensed, general view of what it takes to become a court reporter, and what being a court reporter means. I want to now dive into the "make it" or "break it" dark times that you will come up against from time to time that can be corralled and engineered to work for your benefit if you are ready to address those times. Knowledge is everything. Knowledge can turn a loss or weakness into a win and a strength. Sometimes when your progress seems painfully slow, and you are sure you are never going to get faster on that machine, then it is the time to think about the position you are in and question why. That is why I want to share my learning experiences as a young, struggling court reporting student with you, so YOU can succeed as a court reporter. Oh, learning was fun when it was, "Sue said so," or, phonetically, "Su sed so." That was fun! Then it quickly changed when I opened my Physiology Book.

Parenthetically, "I'm giving you pearls and diamonds now, ladies and gentlemen, pearls and diamonds," says I. Here comes a secret!

MEET DOLLIE DOPPELGANGER, THE VOICE IN MY HEAD

I remember at one point in my schooling having a ghastly time trying to move from 120 wpm (words per minute) to 140 wpm.

I thought, "I have been trying and trying to get out of this speed. I'm stuck and the speedometer won't bulge! What a bummer!"

This was really starting to get me down. And my spirit was down which was bad because I knew how important it was to stay positive, and, well, it wasn't working. I started thinking.

(Familiar voice being heard)

MJ (me): "Oh, oh." (Thinking to myself): "There's the voice in my head again. She's back.

"Pardon me? What did you say?"

THE VOICE: "What is your complaint now?"

MJ: "Well, I am stuck at 120 wpm and not going anywhere!"

THE VOICE: "And what is the magic word, please?"

MJ: "Uh..." (Thinking to myself) "Every time I get in a dither, this Voice comes in my head. Who exactly is this Voice in my head, I wonder? Is she here to shame me?"

THE VOICE: "What is the magic word?"

MJ: "Uh, 'practice', but that isn't working."

THE VOICE: "No, it works, but you need to practice MORE!"

MJ: (Thinking to myself) "This voice is really getting to me! I'm trying to figure out who it is. I started calling her 'Dollie Doppelganger' because she reminds me of me. Is she my doppelganger?

She is very annoying because I can't figure her out, and she always comes when I am down, depressed. She comes at my worst times."

THE VOICE: "You know, you could be a little less irritating. I could help you, but you are being kind of aggravating. Who needs that? You are not taking charge of the problem here and doing something about it!"

MJ: (Hesitating) "Uh, Sorry." (Thinking to myself) "Is she serious? Can't she see my frustration? Is she an apparition? Is she me -- from a parallel universe?"

THE VOICE: (Authoritatively) "MJ, you know what you have to do. You must fluctuate your practice material. You really should know this – I think we covered this before. You need to practice writing more difficult material, you goof. Something like the Congressional Record, like the part where Congress was talking about Zimbabwe, remember? Lots of crazy words in there."

MJ: "I remember - the really hard literary stuff.

"Dictation like this: (Indicating) The Zimbabwe Meeting was attended by Mugabe, ZANU-PF, Morgan Tsvangirai, MDC-Tsvangirai, Ncube, Zimbabwe African People's Union, Kusunoki Mukwazhe."

THE VOICE: "Yes, goofy. You write the African nouns,

you know, the names of the cities and people for 15 minutes, the colloquy of the Congressmen; then go back to 15 minutes of easier stuff, then try to read the steno. Do that for a few times and then again a few more times, then later again, and I guarantee you will break 140 within days."

MJ: *"I think you are right – again."*

THE VOICE: *"Uh-huh. You know this. You were just too lazy to go do it. You KNOW you must practice harder stuff all the time and then do the easier stuff, mix it up, keep it fun and you know that to get better, you must write tougher stuff."*

MJ: *"Uh, yeah, guess so."*

THE VOICE: *"Do I sound familiar?"*

MJ: *"Um, yeah. But, you know, the time it takes to learn all this new stuff like on the spine, the cervical, thorax and lumbar parts and the degenerative disease, and the phalangeal parts, and the acetabulum are all slowing me down while I learn even more abbreviations!"*

THE VOICE: *"Oh, stop! Do you have something against increasing your wealth? Did you think preparing for a super job that*

would increase your standard of living and ocean vacations was going to be a walk in the park? What planet do you come from?"

MJ: "When you put it that way –"

(End of mental exercise)

So, I wanted to share that with you inquiring students-to-be because that voice in my head was actually my mental doppelganger, Dollie. (I gave her that name, but she is really my conscience, talking to me.) I was in a tough spot and my psyche was nudged by my character trait called "Drive" and the voice of my subconscious was my way of reminding myself that I should do what I knew I should do, and Dollie's instruction was exactly what I knew I should do. Get it? Probably not. But it works for me.

We all have an inner voice, and it is the best of ourselves. It is the creed by which we live, our best behavior. When things get hard, difficult, if we think seriously, we can find that voice.

There are times, many times when you will experience frustration and it can cause a feeling of helplessness, but there is a reason for your feelings of anxiety. PLEASE HEAR THIS. You are continuously pushing yourself to perform at higher speeds than you are presently trained to do or presently able to do, but you must have faith in the PROCESS of building that speed, because with REPETITION, (there's that word again!), you WILL achieve a higher speed. It was true when you went from 20 wpm to 40 wpm, 40 wpm to 60 wpm, then 60 wpm to 80 wpm, then 80 to 100, 100 to 120, 120-140, 140-160, 160-180, etc. If you can practice in a court when you are writing 180 wpm, you will really take off and your steno writer will seem to grow wings! You will be "dancing on the keys!" It's all part of a great plan. Believe.

NEVER QUIT!

Faith in yourself is crucial here. Mental toughness is required. I know you can find your own Dollie Doppelganger. You have two choices when you are at the end of your rope in this type of situation: Fight or Flight. Don't take the easy but unsatisfying way out and quit. You may forever regret that decision. Instead, summon your courage to fight harder and make the jump and consult your psyche, your "Dollie" friend, and stay in the ballgame. You are closer to finishing than you know. Oh, and the sweet smell of success will soon be yours to enjoy.

"Do I want to rent or buy my steno writer? "
During your court reporting education, you will be faced with the question of, "Do I rent, or do I buy my steno machine, my writer?" Usually, your chosen school will initially provide you with a writer to use or rent until you start feeling that you must have your own writer.

There are many wonderful companies to choose from. You really should do a search on the Internet, like Google and elsewhere, of all the possible steno writer companies available, how long they have been in business, and attend their shows or podcasts, Zoom, virtual meetings, so that you can gain knowledge of what is available. These companies will go out of their way to assist you. Then you want to make sure the writer you choose is compatible with your laptop or desktop computer for real-time ability.

You must train yourself to write real-time (instant print-out of transcription) if you want to be competitive and be among the best court reporters. An excellent school will provide you with the manner of real-time writing and how to achieve it while you are learning about this fascinating, brilliant system of writing and transcription!

I strongly suggest corroborating with your court reporting friends and acquaintances in your area in discussing what court reporters are on what system and are they happy with that system. You may find yourself working on a "Daily" trial or deposition – meaning instant delivery of testimony that day -- and sharing that with another reporter or reporters. So, if you were all on the same system, that would be very beneficial; however, not mandatory. There are, of course, ways to integrate several systems.

CHAPTER 7

STARTING OUT - PRACTICING IN COURTROOM OR ON DEPOSITIONS

After achieving your Certification, and with ID card in hand, you will want to practice writing on an actual job with another certified court reporter either in a courtroom or in a deposition hearing. It is good to do both so you can gain that experience before you are "on your own, alone on the job."

I started out taking depositions, and until I was able to make my own attorney/client contacts, I free-lanced with a court reporting agency. You will learn who they are by looking in the Yellow Pages, or now more commonly, on the Internet ads, and, most importantly, by networking with the court reporters you are meeting. You will find other court reporters very kind and helpful and willing to assist you because they realize the need to have and help new reporters. They all need substitutes from time to time.

When you can start making your own income, if not before, check into your state and city Court Reporting Associations to acquaint yourself with the history and characteristics of the business in your area. I have already indicated the innumerable advantages that the National Court Reporters Association membership can bring to you throughout the life of your career. It is astonishing.

Chapter 8

ADDITIONAL HELPING AIDS

IN MY SECOND BOOK, I will get into the very helpful aids and ideas that will be of great help in increasing your race to success AND other branches of opportunities now available. Things like:

- Do you know your Civics? Or perhaps the schools do not teach that anymore, or Government. Do you know when new judges will be elected and then take office? Keep up on the judgeships becoming available in your town. They will need a court reporter.

- Network and ask around to see what court reporters need sub reporters the

  most. You can help. And the Per Diem (Payment per day) is very good now.

- Daily Copy

- Travel for an attorney when necessary

- *Your continuing education*

- *Further accomplishments*

- *More and more jobs*

- *Spin-offs from your court reporting career*

CHAPTER 9

BEHAVIOR, MANNERS IN COURT OR A DEPOSITION

Simply, look good, smell good, and write good. You are now an educated professional in a profession of very interesting and talented people, of great ideas, and you are there to help, assist with your knowledge and skill, and to be the humble, silent one most of the time, and always unobtrusive and dignified.

We are wordsmiths. I never stop analyzing new words. Oh, and you'll be great at Scrabble and word games, too, or you probably are already.

CHAPTER 10

THE SIGNED CERTIFICATE

Please read and understand the Certificate that court reporters add as the last page of their transcript of each job, each day of testimony, hearing proceedings, and live by it. Honor it always and honor the oath you take as a court reporter.

My Wish for You!

May you enjoy the highest degree of professionalism in your soon-to-be acquired profession, and may you receive the kind respect of those in the legal field witnessing and benefitting from your hard-to-learn skill, intelligence, and proficiency.

Prepare for your life to be changed, embellished, and blessed! I know you can do it!

My friends, and movers-and-shakers-to-be, I hope in this book I have explained the profession of court reporting to you so that you now have a clearer understanding of the responsibilities and skills a court reporter has and the wonderful expectations that will come, without delving too strongly on the technical part of learning this skill, which you will be more than deluged with in the school of your choice.

Highly qualified certified stenograph court reporters should be able to advance to a position making $100,000 a year and easily upwards of that If one trains for that event to happen RIGHT NOW! A state court reporter, hired by a judge and, thus, the state, has two sources of income : one from the state and a second source from the attorneys on the case who order a transcript from you of the hearing or trial. Remember that. If you are working in a court that is very busy with trials and hearings, you could make much more over your regular salary. Of course, that will push your 40-hour week over many more hours to meet all your deadlines, but that is why I again reiterate, the amount of money you make will be largely dependent on the hard work and thorough application of your learning process now. Be prepared to make your touchdown!

TIME TO GET STARTED!

I hope I have encouraged you to call or visit an NCRA-accredited Court Reporting College to talk to the administrator and find out when you can sign up for their next class. If you have read this far, then you are a wonderful contender for this exhilarating profession!

I believe people are happier when they are learning something new and working towards strong goals. If you are intent on improving your life, your status, and quality of life, this profession will have a tremendous monetary value for you. Indeed, it is worth your time and study to invest yourself in this profession.

You know, just the process alone Improves you so much. You will find your talents and curiosity blossoming. I personally know several friends of mine who were court reporters and became so interested in the law that they became lawyers. Another friend left court reporting after 15 years and became a chiropractor. He was smitten with the medical trials and decided to try chiropractic. Hordes of court reporters eventually opened their own free-lance agency.

There are so many spinoffs to this profession so that you can continue to grow and grow and grow. It is always very interesting and very, very lucrative. The sky to opportunities is wide open.

I know by now you are salivating to begin this winning course of court reporting but let me just end on a philosophical note.

A RHYTHMIC CADENCE OF ITS OWN VITALITY

People are happy when they are being creative. That activity is calming, and people find it also relaxing. There is joy in using the creative art of playing the piano with your hands. There is joy in using the creative art of writing the stenographic code of the Reporter's Record on the Stenograph machine with your hands while simultaneously translating it into English. The ebb and flow of the voices of counsel, coordinated with the movement of your fingers over the keyboard, creates a rhythmic cadence of its own vitality. I like to think of it as my fingers pushing along the Wheels of Justice to a rightful solution.

This realization has stayed with me for almost 45 years. It is what has kept me connected to my best friend, my steno machine, for all that time. The beautiful spirit of that thought is what has enabled my head, body, and hands to continue my fabulous career as a court reporter! I have loved every moment of it, and I have loved meeting all the wonderful, talented people I have had the good fortune to meet along the way. And I have loved possessing this skill that was so hard at times to attain, but I did, and you know now how it is done.

It is yours to possess with self-commitment, with persistence, with perseverance, with tenacity, with the belief that you can do it, with never giving up on yourself. Memorize my Chapter 6, carry it with you. Adopt your own "Dollie," the Voice of your psyche. Your pride in accomplishing this rigorous but extremely interesting ability to write this phenomenally fast testimony and colloquy of the proceedings will take you to new heights you never imagined. I know these "Thoughts for the Soul" will inspire you as they have me!

If imparting my knowledge and expertise I have gathered in this book have been helpful to you in finding your way into this marvelous career, then I am thankful and blessed. I did feel a need to brighten your way along this path and to help you jump over the stumbling blocks of frustration along your way. The decision lies in "your hands".

Believe. Thank you. I wish you all the best of luck!

Let me know how you are doing and of your success in attending a court reporting school and/or finding employment as a court reporter. I am interested in your success. Just drop me a note. You can reach me at my email address of stom37@aol.com. I am so excited for you.

Here's to you, sitting in the court reporter's chair, elevating your income, lifestyle and knowledge!

You can make it happen.

Marijane Stomberg, Author

Former Official and Freelance Court Reporter, CSR, RPR

CHAPTER 11

WOULD YOU LIKE TO EARN A 6-FIGURE INCOME?

I think I already know the answer to that question. As I have explained to you early on, you can do exactly that in a career as a Verbatim Certified Court Reporter. You will be happily taking an abundance of receipts and 1099s substantiating those earnings to your accountant at tax time.

Let me explain how it works. I talked about this earlier, but it needs more explaining. Some District Courts now pay $96,000 or more in salary for a fully certified Verbatim Court Reporter, writing the stenographic method. Such amounts paid are found usually in your larger cities. More people, larger jurisdictions.

Remember when I told you that in doing the work of an Official Court Reporter who is working for a District or Federal Judge, you earn your base salary upon your hiring, which is determined by your having achieved the required certification, competency, and experience.

You also will have an additional income derived from the production of a certified transcript of the Reporter's Record, a printed copy of the hearing or trial which you wrote in stenotype, transcribed via your CAT, proof-read, billed out and delivered to the respective parties; the part of producing the transcript will be done by you, the Independent Contractor. In part, you have become an entrepreneur.

Those transcript fees can add up to another $10,000, $50,000, or $100,000 a year, increasing your livelihood from the basic court income! Yes. You can see how a court reporter today, working in a court requiring a record be made, can earn - including her base salary and additional transcript fees - up to $200,000 a year. That may not be happening every year, but many. This happens in courts where there is a large number of cases tried, that may have attorneys wanting every part of the trial transcribed, oftentimes on a Daily Copy Real-Time basis, which are charged at higher rates, and also in trials in the bigger cities, like Houston, New York City, Los Angeles, to name just a few.

Where do court reporters get paid the most?

Court reporter salaries also tend to differ quite a bit based on their location. **New York's** court reporters earn the highest average salary in the U.S., at $96,640 ($46.46/hour) according to the BLS, followed by those in California, who earned an average salary of $89,120 ($42.85/hour) during this time.

NOTE: This does not include the amount for transcript orders, so add that to the amount shown. In some cases, it will double.

In the celebrity cases, or those of high national interest, like the OJ Simpson case, because they were long trials with many copies being ordered, I imagine those court reporters working on the trial probably made over a million dollars. I never saw their paychecks, so I do not know the exact amount. I am surmising, if you will, and I have read that fact.

Only the best proven verbatim court reporters will earn that. That is why I implored you in the beginning of this book to train and work smart, work your hardest, be prepared for the ultimate success. It is determined right now as you pick up the steno machine and pledge, "I am going to do this and reach for the top!"

If you want to become a Registered Professional Reporter, offered by NCRA, you will need to pass their test, which is very similar to the CSR exam you will take, but all this will be explained to you when you are in school.

However, for your information, the following is wonderful knowledge to have when going through the throes of becoming a Certified Verbatim Court Reporter.

I am incorporating here information from the Texas Court System for you. I show the Texas information because Texas is the state where I spent most of my reporting career, although all the states now share the same or very similar information.

https://www.txcourts.gov/jbcc/court-reporters-certification/frequently-asked-questions/

Certification & Registration

1. What are the requirements to become a Texas court reporter?

You are required to:
1. have a high school diploma or GED equivalent,
2. pass the state certification exam, and
3. pass a state and federal criminal history background check.

The exam consists of:
4. part A (the skills portion) and
5. part B (the written knowledge portion).

Texas does not allow passing the skills exam in "legs"; the literary, jury charge, and Q&A portions of the exam must all be passed at the same time. Please refer to the Exam page of our website for details on the exam and the Initial Certification page of our website for additional details on certification. Refer also to the FAQ regarding criminal history requirements for certification.

2. How do I know if I need to register my firm; what is the definition of a firm?

3. How do I register my court reporting firm with the Commission?

4. If I have a criminal history, can I be a court reporter?

If there is an incident in your past that you are concerned may cause a problem with your becoming a Texas CSR, and you are enrolled or planning to enroll in court reporting school or planning to take the certification exam, you may first request a criminal history evaluation letter from the JBCC. Under section 3.5 of the JBCC Rules, you may request a criminal history evaluation letter by a written request in which you state the basis for your potential ineligibility. The Commission will notify you in writing of its determination. If you wish to sit for the exam before a determination has been made you may do so, with the understanding that even if you pass the exam a certification will not be issued until the Commission makes a determination on your eligibility status, and that a refund of the exam/application fees will not be issued. Also, if you take the exam and the Commission then determines you are not eligible, you will not receive a refund of the application and exam fees.

5. Am I required to attend court reporting school, or have a degree, to become a CSR?

The Commission does not require attendance at a court reporting school, nor a degree, to become a CSR. Please refer to the Initial Certification page of our website for information on the requirements to become a court reporter.

6. Are Texas CSR's also required to be notaries?

No.

7. My certification or registration has expired. How can I be reinstated?

8. Does Texas offer reciprocity or endorsements for out-of-state reporters?

9. If I am out of state, but choose to maintain my Texas CSR certification , what must I do?

10. When do certifications and registrations expire?

11. How do I update the Supervisor for my Apprentice Certification?

12. Are apprentice certification applicants required to submit proof of good standing?

13. If I apply to for an apprentice certification and pass all parts of the oral exam at one time, am I automatically issued a full certification? Is my apprentice application fee refunded?

Continuing Education

1. How many hours of continuing education are required to renew?

You must obtain 10 hours over your 2-year certification period. Of that 2 1/2 hours must be in ethics, Texas rules, or both.

Effective 04/12/2018, under section 6.9 (a) of the JBCC Rules, a certified court reporter may carry forward to the next certification period up to 4 hours of approved continuing education. Special category CE (i.e., ethics/rules) cannot be carried forward.

2. Can you tell me how many hours I have?

3. Can you tell me if the course I'm taking will count towards the CE requirements? How can I get a list of approved CE courses?

4. If a program is approved by NCRA will the Commission accept it?

If you wish to use an NCRA approved program towards your CE requirements, you must submit an application for course approval. You must apply for course approval through the online certification and licensing system. Refer to the pdf Guide to Using the Online System, located on the home page of our website, for instructions on how to apply for CE approval.

5. Do course approval applications need to be submitted before attending the program?

6. Once a course approval application is received by the Commission, how long before it is approved?

7. Can I have the (CE) requirement waived for my upcoming renewal?

There are no provisions in rule to waive the CE requirement.

8. May I use articles or books to satisfy the Texas court reporter CE requirements?

9. If I take an online NCRA program will I receive full CE credit for my Texas certification?

10. What is the fee to apply for course approval?

11. How do I report the CE courses I've taken?

12. Do I need to obtain CE for my provisional certification?

CSR Examination

1. Who administers the Certified Shorthand Reporters (CSR) examination?

The CSR examination is currently administered by the Texas Court Reporters Association (TCRA) on behalf of the Commission. Please refer to TCRA's website for questions regarding exam registration, exam fees, scores, etc.

2. What dictionary is used for grading the exam?

Currently the Eleventh Edition of Merriam Webster's Collegiate Dictionary. This is subject to change, so check with the vendor prior to taking the exam.

3. What do I do if I need special accommodations under the American's with Disabilities Act?

4. Can I use a paperless steno machine?

Yes. You are not required to use paper notes, but you are strongly encouraged to use them in the event you have equipment failure and can no longer access your notes electronically. Please be advised that only the final paper transcript is accepted for grading purposes. If you cannot turn in a transcript you will receive a failing grade.

5. If I want to test under two methods, machine and stenomask, what are my options?

You must pass the oral exam for each method. If you have previously taken and passed the written exam, you do not need to retake it, but you do need to note on your paperwork that you have passed it, when you passed it, and the file number you tested under when you passed it.

6. Where is the CSR exam held?

Please refer to the website for the Texas Court Reporters Association for this information since they administer the certification exam on behalf of the Commission.

7. Do you have to qualify to take the oral exam?

Effective September 01, 2019, the JBCC no longer requires you to qualify to sit for the oral exam. Please refer to the Exam page of our website for information on exam requirements.

8. How long does an exam regrade take?

9. How will I know I am registered to sit for the exam?

10. Can examinees write in real time?

Yes.

11. When will I know my exam results? When will I get my certification?

Test results will be provided according to the timeline established in Rule 3.11 of the JBCC Rules. Test results are not provided by phone, fax, or to third parties. Certification cards will be issued by regular mail after the Supreme Court certifies the names of the successful examinees.

12. Where can I obtain the forms for the exam?

13. If I passed part of the exam before do I need to take it again?

Effective 09/01/17, per section 152.201 (c-1) of Chapter 152 and section 3.11 (d) of the JBCC Rules, passing exam scores are valid for a period of 2 years after the date of the examination. If you've not become certified within 2 years of passing the exam, you must retake the exam passed. Per section 6.2 (g)(3) of the JBCC Rules, you would not have to retake the exam passed if the scores have not expired. See Exam Results section of the Exam page of our website for additional information.

14. How do I request a regrade or review of my exam?

15. Can the notes from my dictation be used when grading my exam?

They can be viewed in circumstances when something is in question and to determine if someone cheated, but they cannot be considered when determining grades. The final (printed) transcript is the only document that will be used to determine whether an examinee passed or failed the CSR exam.

Renewals

1. Can I submit my course approval applications at the same time I submit my renewal?

2. What is the refund process for renewal fees?

3. My certification has been expired for 1 year or more. I have been living out of state. How do I become recertified in Texas?

You may become recertified without examination only if you meet the following criteria:

1. You were certified in Texas prior to moving out of state;
2. You are currently certified in the other state;
3. You have been practicing court reporting in the other state for a period of at least 1 year preceding the date of application for recertification in Texas; and,
4. Your certification is currently in good standing.

If you meet the above criteria you may become

recertified in Texas by following the procedures below:

5. Submit the renewal application and submit copies of your CE documentation (i.e., copies of your certificates of attendance).
6. Submit all required paperwork to the Commission (along with documentation confirming the above four criteria) with the appropriate renewal fee(s). Please refer to section 3.2 (g) of the JBCC Rules for details.
7. Pay to the commission a fee that is equal to twice the normally required renewal fee.

If you do not meet the criteria above, please refer to the Initial Certification page of our website for information on becoming reinstated.

4. Are extensions granted for renewals?

1.
2.
3.

5. Can I put my new expiration date on my certificates even though I have not received my new certification?

6. Where can I get forms to renew my certification?

7. How do I know when my certification expires?

8. Can I use my credit card to pay for my renewal and just email or fax my renewal documents?

9. Can I send in part of my renewal paperwork before I expire and the rest later, to ensure I meet the deadline?

10. Will you accept a check from my county for my renewal fees?

11. How do I find out the name of the seminar I attended?

12. When am I considered renewed?

Miscellaneous

1. Have you received my paperwork? Can you check on the status of my paperwork?

2. What pitch must I use on my transcripts?

3. How do I change my name with the Commission?

4. How do I change my address with the Commission?

5. Why does the Commission have strict deadline(s)?

6. Is a court reporter's home address or home or personal telephone number available to the public if requested?

7. How long must we keep our notes?

8. Do the JBCC Rules apply to other states or federal courts?

9. When are applications considered received by the Commission?

10. How do I find a court reporter or court reporting firm?

11. How do I order another certification card or wall certificate?

12. How do I update the ownership of my business entity?

(End of the Texas courts information)

WHAT ABOUT FIRMS ?

You may have noticed information in the above information about court reporting firms. Does owning your own firm interest you? Perhaps not now, but after you have worked as a court reporter for a while, or even before, you may become very interested. I have known several industrious friends who have been highly successful in launching their own firm.

Once they worked in the field, were aware of all the ins and outs of the business, the demands OF and the demands FOR, and the income that could be made by taking on the work and embellishment of the work's rewards, they decided to begin their own firm, hiring their own court reporters and by supplying jobs for them, would work with them on a 30-40% commission basis, depending on whether they needed further training. The percentage there is probably negotiable often, according to each individual case.

If you have such a well-developed, well-run firm, you can make over a million dollars, plus much more. It depends on the number on staff of court reporters you have, the Videotaped Deposition business, the Zoom availability, your established reputation of quality, dependability, and competence of staff.

So, there you can see where studying the science of court reporting can take you. It has become a science.

Court reporting started out years ago using a stenographer, writing what we comically call, "chicken scratching," but more properly was named Gregg Shorthand or Pitman Shorthand.

Then it evolved into the nomenclature of a court stenographer.

Then the legal world realized they must have a verbatim transcription of notes in order to be able to rely on the sworn to tell the truth testimony being offered for the judge or jury to consider, and later to the appellate court; thereby utilizing and demanding the competency and speed by the stenographic performance of the Certified Verbatim CAT (Computer-Aided Transcription) Court Reporter-Technician. Indeed, court reporters have morphed into technicians, also. We must set up and understand our writer, possess the ability of broadcasting what we are writing on that real-time machine to the judge, the attorneys, jury, and others, and, lastly, set up a Zoom scenario, broadcasting and supporting a virtual meeting, conference with others outside of our offices. So, yes, we are court reporter-technicians.

Yes, computers finally made it into the court reporting business in a big way. No more, the dictating system of talking on tapes covering all the matters of the court or depositions and working with smearing, carbon copies, thought now to be antiquated and archaic, and unsatisfactory, but it was all we had.

REAL-TIME DELIVERY ARRIVES!

Stenographic CAT companies sprouted up to transport us into the 21st Century, alleviating time-consuming methods of the slow production of needed transcripts, and instead, giving us the electronic tools to produce quick answers for the exuberant judges, attorneys, and parties.

Companies like Stenograph, ProCat, Diamente sell writers and laptops for real-time translation, and there are many more to view if you google them and see the market. Another outstanding court reporting school is:

Mark Kislingbury Academy in Houston for court reporting and captioners. They are located mainly in Houston and are a great source of information.

* * *

At this point, I would like to insert similar information about the State of California's rules on the Certification of Court Reporters there, although not in as much volume as for Texas. It is good for you to have a variance.

Eligibility for Examination

The eligibility requirements are as follows (Section 8020, Business & Professions Code):

- (1) Over 18 years of age;

- (2) high school education or its equivalent;

- (3) has not committed any acts or crimes constituting grounds for denial of licensure and

- (4) the applicant must submit satisfactory evidence that he or she has originally obtained one of the following:

(a) 12 months of full-time work experience in *making* verbatim records of hearings, or judicial or related proceedings by means of machine shorthand writing *and transcribing* such records. Only records of multiple-voice proceedings, such as court and deposition proceedings, will be considered in calculating the required hours. Time spent in transcribing taped recordings or in reporting lectures, etc., will not be considered. A letter from an employer, on their business letterhead, signed by the official in charge, is required when submitting your application as proof of your experience. If you are a freelance reporter or have owned your own business, three letters from clients you have worked for will be required. Letters should list date of employment, whether it was full-time or part-time, your duties, and what percentage of time was spent in each of those duties. In addition, job/work sheets documenting at least 1400 hours will be required. Each job sheet or work sheet should indicate the kind of job reported and the number of hours actually spent reporting.

(b) A verified certificate of satisfactory completion of a prescribed course of study from a **CALIFORNIA RECOGNIZED COURT REPORTING SCHOOL**, or certification from such school evidencing equivalent proficiency, and of the ability to make a verbatim record of material dictated in accordance with regulations adopted by the board contained in Title 16 of the California Code of Regulations.

(c) A National Court Reporters Association RPR Certificate or Certificate of Merit or National Verbatim Reporters Association CVR Certificate stating the original issuance date of the certificate.

IMPORTANT PLEASE NOTE:

SPECIAL ATTENTION MUST BE GIVEN TO INSTRUCTIONS REGARDING QUALIFYING DOCUMENTS AS THESE ARE VITAL IN DETERMINING ELIGIBILITY. SIGNATURES VERIFYING EMPLOYMENT, SUCCESSFUL COMPLETION OF A COURSE OF STUDY, OR ANY OTHER QUALIFYING METHOD MUST BE AN ORIGINAL.

Incomplete documents will be returned. All documents must be submitted to the Board *no later than the announced final filing date.* For purposes of determining the date upon which an application is deemed filed, the date of postmark affixed by the United States Postal Service (not a postage meter), or the date certified by a bona fide private courier service on the envelope containing the application shall prevail.

DON'T PROCRASTINATE!

Mail your application early. Don't you be the one person applying for this exam that is denied because the application is postmarked one day too late.

DENIAL OF A LICENSE

Applicants, who have been convicted of a crime other than minor traffic citations, must disclose the matter, in detail, as requested on the application form, for consideration by the Board. Matters sealed or expunged under California penal Code Section 1203.4 are not exempt; they must be listed. For each offense, the Board requires certified copies from the court or other appropriate agency of all the following:

- (1) Court sentencing order showing final charge and penalties and/or sanctions, and

- (2) Court document showing that all sentences, sanctions, fines, etc., have been satisfied.

If the applicant is still on probation, a letter from the probation office stating the applicant's status and progress may be substituted for item 2 above if no other sanctions were imposed.

Privacy Policy

- https://www.courtreportersboard.ca.gov is designed, developed, and maintained to be in compliance with California Government Code Sections 7405 and 11135. Consistent with the Web Content Accessibility Guidelines 2.0, published by the Web Accessibility Initiative of the World Wide Web Consortium, the undersigned certify conformance at a Level AA standard or higher.

- Signature on file

    Jason Piccione Date

- Chief Information Officer

    California Department of Consumer Affairs

Copyright © 2022 State of California

(End of California information)

WHAT A COURT REPORTER IS NOT!

Next, as it becomes clearer how intricate and diversified the life of a court reporter is, let me tell you what it is not.

A court reporter is NOT a glorified secretary, whose highest proficiency required is 80 to 120 wpm. I'm being facetious. Secretaries are an important part of the business world and I used to be one. I loved it but it could not afford to me the lifestyle I yearned for.

A court reporter is not a legal secretary.

A court reporter is not a paralegal.

A court reporter is not a court clerk.

A court reporter is not a license clerk.

A court reporter is not a medical transcriptionist.

A court reporter IS a highly-trained, highly-skilled reporter who writes verbatim The Record for the court's matters requiring a record, for the attorneys involved requesting it, also, and is the one who is responsible for protecting the Record by acting upon the oath to provide a verbatim record required.

OFFSHOOTS DERIVED FROM COURT REPORTING

CAPTIONING: Marvelous for the deaf and hard of hearing as the "signers" come to their aid.

Court reporters provide an accurate description of court proceedings.

Court reporters create word-for-word transcriptions at trials, depositions, administrative hearings, and other legal proceedings. Simultaneous captioners provide similar transcriptions for television or for presentations in other settings, such as press conferences and business meetings, for people who are deaf or hard of hearing.

Duties

Court reporters and simultaneous captioners typically do the following:

- Attend depositions, hearings, proceedings, and other events that require verbatim transcripts
- Capture spoken dialogue with special equipment, such as stenography machines and digital recording devices
- Report speakers' identification, gestures, and actions
- Read or play back portions of events or legal proceedings upon request
- Ask speakers to clarify inaudible statements or testimony
- Review notes they have taken, including the spelling of names and technical terminology
- Provide copies of transcripts and recordings to the parties involved
- Transcribe television or movie dialogue for the benefit of viewers
- Provide real-time transcription of presentations in public forums for people who are deaf or hard of hearing

Court reporters have a critical role in legal proceedings, which require an exact record of what occurred. These workers are responsible for producing a complete, accurate, and secure transcript of depositions, trials, and other legal proceedings. The official record allows <u>judges</u> and <u>lawyers</u> to efficiently search for important information contained in the transcript. Court reporters also index and catalog exhibits used during legal proceedings.

Simultaneous captioners primarily serve people who are deaf or hard of hearing by transcribing speech to text.

Court reporters and simultaneous captioners typically do the following:

- Attend depositions, hearings, proceedings, and other events that require verbatim transcripts
- Capture Court reporters have a critical role in legal proceedings, which require an exact record of what occurred. These workers are responsible for producing a complete, accurate, and secure transcript of depositions, trials, and other legal proceedings. The official record allows judges and lawyers to efficiently search for

important information contained in the transcript. Court reporters also index and catalog exhibits used during legal proceedings.

Simultaneous captioners primarily serve people who are deaf or hard of hearing by transcribing speech to text as the speech occurs. They typically work in settings other than courtrooms or law offices.

The following are examples of types of simultaneous captioners:

Broadcast captioners provide transcriptions for television programs (called closed captions). They capture dialogue for displaying to television viewers, primarily those who are deaf or hard of hearing. Some broadcast captioners may transcribe dialogue in real time during broadcasts; others caption during the program's postproduction.

Communication access real-time translation (CART) providers work primarily with people who are deaf or hard of hearing during meetings, doctors' appointments, and other situations requiring real-time transcription. For example, CART providers may caption the dialogue of college classes and present an immediate transcript to students who are learning English as a second language.

Although some simultaneous captioners accompany their clients to events, many broadcast captioners and CART providers do not. Establishing remote access allows these workers to hear and type dialogue without having to be physically present in the room.

Court reporters and simultaneous captioners turn dialogue into text for a variety of audiences. For information about workers who convey dialogue through sign language, cued speech, or other means to people who are deaf or hard of hearing, see the profile on interpreters and translators.

Court reporters and simultaneous captioners use different methods for recording speech, such as stenotype machines, steno masks, and digital recording devices.

Stenotype machines work like keyboards but create words through key combinations rather than single characters, allowing court reporters to keep up with fast-moving dialog.

Excerpt below taken from the U.S. Bureau of Labor Statistics: "Court Reporters and Simultaneous Captioners:

"Court Reporters create word-for-word transcription at trials, depositions, and other legal proceedings. Simultaneous captioners provide similar transcriptions for television or for other presentations in other settings, such as press conferences and business meetings, for people who are deaf or hard of hearing.

"Most court reporters work in courts or legislatures; simultaneous captioners may work from their home or central office. Some court reporters and simultaneous captioners travel to other locations such as meeting sites or public events."

"The median annual wage for court reporters and simultaneous captioners was $60,380 in May 2021. The highest 10% earned more than $103,270."

That is from the U.S. Bureau of Labor Statistics.

That is in line with what I have been stating. The highest 10% most likely were working in the District Courts or Federal Courts, whether they were official reporters or free-lance reporters. Remember, too, what I told you about the 2nd income reporters make from the transcript they produce as independent contractors, ordered, and paid for by attorneys. That is not included here. It all makes sense.

In Texas there are many types of courts of record requiring a court reporter to be reporting matters in the courtroom: Civil and Criminal District Courts, County Courts, County-at-Law Courts. Court structure and court names vary from state to state.

It is important to point out the expenses one will incur in deciding to seek entering the profession of a court reporter.

First, you will have tuition to pay at a specified, chosen qualified school. This varies, but one school might charge approximately $575 a month, or $6,900 a year. Another could be higher or lower. Or, many junior colleges offer courses in this field, for an 8-week semester of 4 or $500. You will need to google this information to find out the specific school that meets your circumstances.

Note: I have covered much of this previously.

You can certainly complete the necessary work

in two years or less as I have stated before. I can tell you, it is worth it. This profession does not require a 4-year college degree or a $40,000 a year investment, totaling for the usual 4 years, $160,000! You just must get that speed up and understand your textbook, be thorough and determined, and you will make it into a thriving profession.

JUST DO IT!1

MY HUMBLE REQUEST!

Thank You For Reading My Book!

I really appreciate all your feedback and

I love hearing what you have to say.

I need your input to make my next Court Reporting book and future books better.

Please leave me a helpful review on Amazon, letting me know what you thought of the book.

I strove for excellence in jarring you into the betterment of YOU so YOU may enjoy your pursuit of happiness in life's best form!

Thanks so much.

Marijane Stomberg, Author

Made in the USA
Monee, IL
01 July 2024

61042414R00056